4,1

Children's Authors

Laura Ingalls Wilder

Mae Woods
ABDO Publishing Company

visit us at
www.abdopub.com

Published by ABDO Publishing Company, 4940 Viking Drive, Suite 622, Edina, Minnesota
55435. Copyright © 2000 Abdo Consulting Group, Inc., Pentagon Tower, P.O. Box 36036,
Minneapolis, Minnesota 55435 USA. International copyrights reserved in all countries. No part
of this book may be reproduced in any form without written permission from the publisher.

Printed in the United States.

Photos: Laura Ingalls Wilder Home Association, AP/Wideworld
Editors: Bob Italia, Tamara L. Britton, Kate A. Furlong
Art Direction: Pat Laurel

Library of Congress Cataloging-in-Publication Data

Woods, Mae.
   Laura Ingalls Wilder / Mae Woods.
     p. cm. -- (Children's authors)
   Summary: Recounts the life story of the author of the "Little House" books, from her
childhood in Wisconsin to her old age at Rocky Ridge Farm.
   Includes bibliographical references (p.) and index.
   ISBN 1-57765-113-8
   1. Wilder, Laura Ingalls, 1867-1957--Juvenile literature. 2. Authors, American--20th
century--Biography--Juvenile literature. 3. Frontier and pioneer life--United
States--Juvenile literature. 4. Children's stories--Authorship--Juvenile literature. [1.
Wilder, Laura Ingalls, 1867-1957. 2. Authors, American. 3. Frontier and pioneer life.] I.
Title.

PS3545.I342 Z975 2000
813.'52--dc21
[B]   99-088858

Contents

Pioneer Days

When Laura Ingalls was born, the American West was a great **wilderness**. The government gave land to anyone brave enough to tame it. Many families left their homes and set out to build new ones in the West. These settlers were known as pioneers.

Laura was one of hundreds of pioneer girls. As pioneers, Laura and her family faced **hardships** and danger. But they kept moving forward. Through their hard work, the Ingalls family made a new life for themselves on the **frontier**.

During her 90-year lifetime, Laura saw the United States grow and change. Towns, farms, and highways covered up the vast, empty **prairies** of her childhood. So, she decided to write down her stories of the pioneer days so they would not be forgotten. Through Laura's words, her family lives on and teaches lessons in courage, faith, and love.

Laura Ingalls Wilder

The Ingalls Family

*L*aura Elizabeth Ingalls was born on February 7, 1867. Her parents were Charles and Caroline Ingalls. She called her mother "Ma" and her father "Pa." Laura had an older sister named Mary. She had two younger sisters named Carrie and Grace.

The Ingalls family moved many times during Laura's childhood. Pa knew his family could live anywhere as long as there was fresh water, good soil, and animals to hunt.

Pa was a skilled **carpenter**. He built their houses and furniture. Pa was also an excellent fiddle player who knew hundreds of songs. He loved to laugh and share a good story. Ma taught the girls to read and sew. All the girls helped Ma cook and clean.

Laura loved each little house her family settled in. But she came to understand that home is simply where your family is at the moment. "Home" might even be a covered wagon traveling west.

The Ingalls family (left to right): Ma, Carrie, Laura, Pa, Grace, and Mary

House on the Prairie

*L*aura's story begins in the Big Woods of Wisconsin, where she was born. Laura did not live in the Big Woods for long. Before she was two, Pa decided to move the family west. The Ingalls family packed their belongings into a covered wagon and started their journey.

Two horses drew their wagon across the land. The family's bulldog, Jack, trotted beside them. Each night they set up camp, cooked their meals, and slept under the stars.

The Ingalls family settled in Missouri. But they did not stay there long! Pa wanted to move to the **prairies** of Montgomery County, Kansas.

On the prairie, Pa found a beautiful spot near a creek. Then he built a log cabin and a **stable**. Laura's sister Carrie was born in this cabin in 1870.

The Ingalls family soon faced problems. They had settled on Native American land. The Native Americans wanted the new settlers to leave. The government decided that the Native Americans had rights to the land. So, the Ingalls family left Kansas.

They returned to the Big Woods of Wisconsin. Laura's family moved back into their old house. Laura and Mary started to go to school. The girls got to spend lots of time with their relatives.

Soon, Pa wanted to move west again. So, the family packed their belongings and started out on another journey.

Laura and her family journeyed west in a covered wagon.

Plum Creek

*T*he Ingalls family decided to settle near Walnut Grove, Minnesota. Their first house was a **dugout** built into a hill. It was near Plum Creek.

Laura loved playing in the creek. Once the current pulled her down and she nearly drowned. But Laura wasn't afraid of the water.

Life was going well for the Ingalls family. Pa built a new house and planted a large wheat crop. The Ingalls family joined the church in Walnut Grove. And Mary and Laura started going to school.

But the Ingalls' good fortune did not last long. Before the **harvest**, swarms of grasshoppers appeared. They ate everything, including Pa's crops.

Pa traveled east to find work. When he returned, the family moved into a house in town. That fall, Laura's little brother Charles Frederick was born. His sisters called him Freddie.

In the spring, the family moved back to their house on Plum Creek. Pa tried to raise another wheat crop. But the eggs from the last year's grasshoppers hatched. Grasshoppers destroyed Pa's crops again.

Pa decided it was time to move on. The Ingalls family traveled to Wabasha County, Minnesota. Then baby Freddie got sick and died. The family decided to move on to Burr Oak, Iowa. Laura's sister Grace was born there.

Carrie, Mary, and Laura Ingalls

The Ingalls family stayed in Burr Oak for a short time. Then they returned to Walnut Grove. All the girls except Laura fell ill with scarlet fever. The disease caused Mary to go blind.

Silver Lake

Pa was offered a job at a railroad camp in De Smet in the Dakota Territory. This time, Pa moved first and his family followed later.

Ma, Mary, Laura, Carrie, and Grace rode the train from Walnut Grove to Tracy. They traveled the rest of the way to De Smet by wagon.

During their travels to De Smet, Laura described everything she saw to Mary. Laura had learned to "see" things with words in order to share her world with her blind sister.

In De Smet, Pa had selected a piece of land near Silver Lake. He built a house and planted cottonwood trees. He also built a store in town, which he planned to sell.

The new little house was cozy in the evenings. The girls made popcorn in the fireplace. Pa played his fiddle and sang as Ma sewed. Sometimes Ma read them stories or letters.

As railroads stretched west, they created many new jobs for workers like Pa.

Town Life

*T*he Dakota winters were fierce. Pa decided the family should live in town. At first, Laura was unhappy. She felt **awkward** around strangers. But Laura soon made friends at school. She was a good student and could play ball as well as any of the boys.

The 1880-1881 winter was long and difficult. **Blizzards** raged for seven months. Snow blocked the railroad tracks. The store ran out of food and **fuel**. Laura and Ma ground wheat in a coffee mill and used it to make bread. When the Ingalls ran out of wood, they twisted hay into bundles and burned them.

In May, the snow finally melted enough for a train to bring in supplies and mail. There was a large **barrel** for the Ingalls family. It had Christmas presents and a turkey. So, Laura and her family had a very special Christmas dinner in the spring!

Laura worked hard in school. She liked English, history, and poetry.

Laura Grows Up

Laura wanted to earn money so Mary could go to a college for blind students. So, Laura worked as a **seamstress** and studied for her teacher's **certificate**. During this time she also met a young **homesteader** named Almanzo Wilder.

In 1883, Laura earned her teaching certificate. While she was still a high school student, Laura began teaching at the Bouchie School.

The Bouchie School was far from the Ingalls' home. So, she moved in with the Bouchie family. Almanzo drove his sleigh through the cold and snow to bring Laura home on the weekends.

In 1885, Laura and Almanzo got married. They farmed some land near De Smet. A year later, Laura and Almanzo had their first child, Rose.

The young Wilder family soon faced problems. **Droughts**, storms, and grasshoppers destroyed their crops year after year. Their house and barn burned down. And Almanzo and Laura caught **diphtheria**, which left Almanzo **crippled**. Then in 1889, they had a son who died shortly after his birth.

Laura and Almanzo Wilder shortly after their wedding

In the spring of 1890, Laura and Almanzo decided to leave De Smet. They moved to Westville, Florida. The warm weather helped Almanzo's health. But Laura was unhappy. After two years, they returned to De Smet.

Soon, the Wilders again left their family and friends. This time they moved to the **Ozarks**. They claimed a **homestead** near Mansfield, Missouri, in 1894. They called it Rocky Ridge Farm. They lived there happily for the rest of their days.

Laura Writes Her Story

*L*aura's daughter Rose grew up hearing about her parents' early days. She knew her mom's stories would entertain children and teach them about pioneer life. Rose encouraged her mom to write her family's history.

After talking to Rose, Laura said, "I began to think what a wonderful childhood I had had. How I had seen the whole frontier, the woods, the Indian country of the great plains, the frontier towns, the building of the railroads in wild, unsettled country, **homesteading** and farmers coming in . . . I had seen and lived it all."

Laura was 65 years old when she started to write books about her family. Her first book was *Little House in the Big Woods*. It was a **Newbery Honor Book** in 1932.

Laura wrote six more books about her family's pioneer days. She also wrote *Farmer Boy*, a book about Almanzo's life as a boy on a New York farm.

Even after the success of Laura's books, the Wilders continued to farm Rocky Ridge for many years.

Laura's Fame

*A*fter her first book was published in 1932, Laura quickly became famous. Hundreds of children wrote letters to her. The Children's Library Association created an award in her name. And in 1974, her books inspired the long-running television show, *Little House on the Prairie*.

Even though Laura grew famous, she and Almanzo made few changes in their lives. They continued to work the farm and enjoy the simple pleasures of country life. In 1949, Almanzo died at the age of 92. Laura continued to live at Rocky Ridge Farm until she passed away in 1957.

Today, the "Little House" series continues to delight new readers. The books are filled with adventure, humor, and drama. They are a bright, memorable **portrait** of the pioneer spirit in America.

At age 85, Laura signs copies of her books for fans in Springfield, Missouri.

Glossary

awkward - clumsy or easily embarrassed.

barrel - a large, rounded wooden container.

blizzard - a heavy snowstorm with strong, cold winds.

carpenter - a person who builds and repairs things made of wood.

certificate - a paper that says someone has fulfilled the requirements to practice in a certain field, such as teaching.

crippled - when a person loses the full use of his or her arms or legs.

diphtheria - a disease that affects the throat and can cause death.

drought - a long period of dry weather.

dugout - a shelter dug into the ground or in a hillside.

frontier - the border between settled land and wilderness.

fuel - something that is burned to give heat.

hardship - the cause of difficulties, pain, or suffering.

harvest - the process of gathering a crop when it becomes ripe.

homestead - a piece of land the U.S. government gave to pioneers who were willing to settle it.

Newbery Award - an award given by the American Library Association to the author of the year's best children's book. Books that are runners-up are called Newbery Honor Books.

Ozarks - a forested group of highlands in Missouri, Arkansas, and Oklahoma.

portrait - a description, drawing, painting, or photograph.

prairie - a large area of flat land with grass and few trees.

stable - a barn.

seamstress - a woman who sews clothes.

wilderness - a wild place where no people live.

Internet Sites

Laura Ingalls Wilder, Frontier Girl

http://webpages.marshall.edu/~irby1/laura/index.html

This kid-friendly site lets you read about Laura Ingalls Wilder's life, listen to music that Pa played on his fiddle, and view photographs of Laura's friends, family, and homes. This site also has a Frontier Kids' Page with paper topics.

Laura Ingalls Wilder Home & Museum

http://www.bestoftheozarks.com/

wilderhome/

This is the official site of Laura Ingalls Wilder's Rocky Ridge home and farm. It has information about the home in which the Little House books were written.

Laura Ingalls Wilder at Rocky Ridge Farm

Index